AF176475

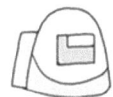

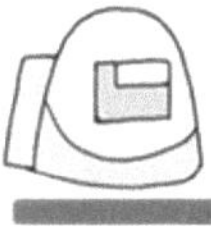

Crewape

You couldn't have seen me in the vents

Mr.T

But I did

Crewape

I went into the vents when nobody was there!

Ricky Roogle

Cartoons, Memes and Jokes

for Am@ng.us Fans

Bibliografische Information der Deutschen Nationalbibliothek:
Die Deutsche Nationalbibliothek verzeichnet diese Publikation in der
Deutschen Nationalbibliografie; detaillierte bibliografische
Daten sind im Internet über http://dnb.dnb.de abrufbar.

Herstellung und Verlag: BoD – Books on Demand, Norderstedt
ISBN: 9783752658453

**How I feel when I am the one
who exposed the impostor and was right
from the start.**

„I'am God."

Types of headaches

Migraine

Hypertension

Stress

**Your teammates
trusting the
Impostor more than you**

Impostor surrounded

Care instructions for a mini crewmate

HOW GAMERS ARE SLEEPING

PUBG
GAMER

FIFA
GAMER

MINECRAFT
GAMER

AMONG US
GAMER

ZZZ

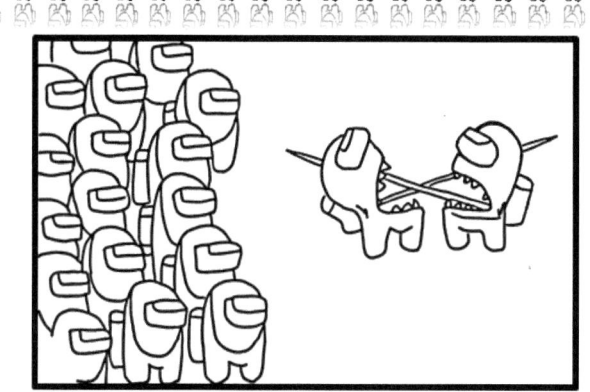

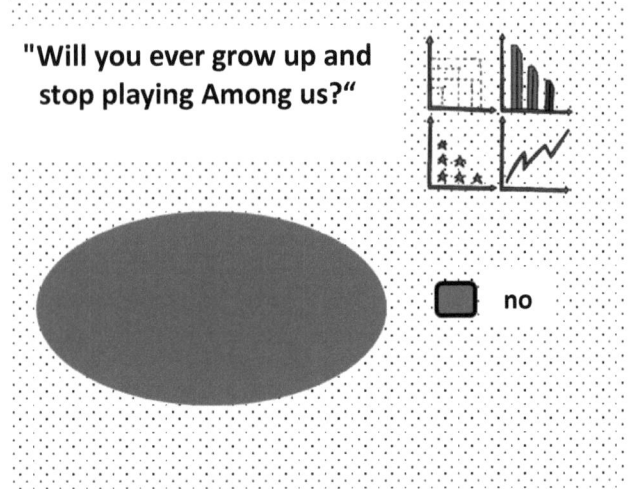

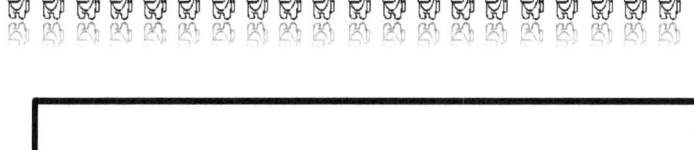

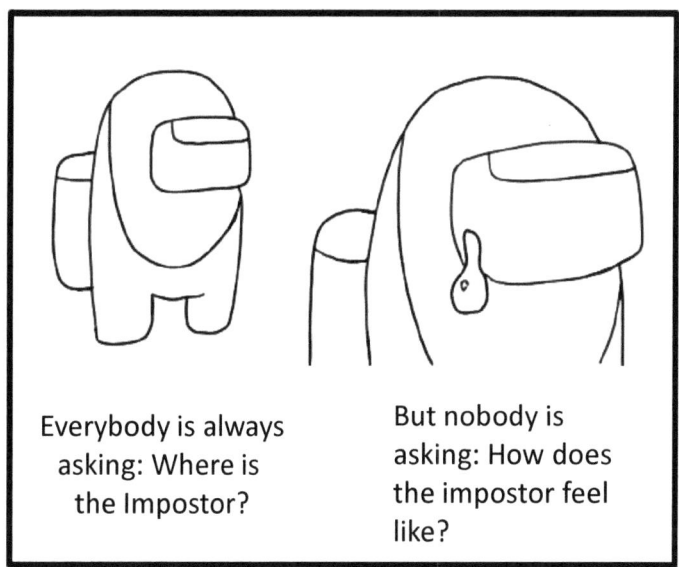

Mini crewmates during the Emergency meetings

12 years old nowadays

The moment when you are doing a task and you notice the vents being opened behind you.

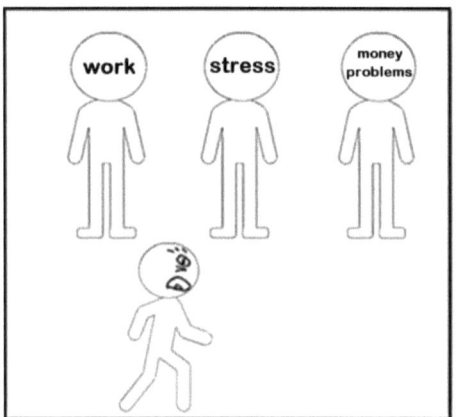

You know you are a true Among us fan, if you know 'The Skeld' better than your neighborhood.

And here is the truth about the violent death of Bob:

Signpost discovered on Polus:

Noobs in Among Us:

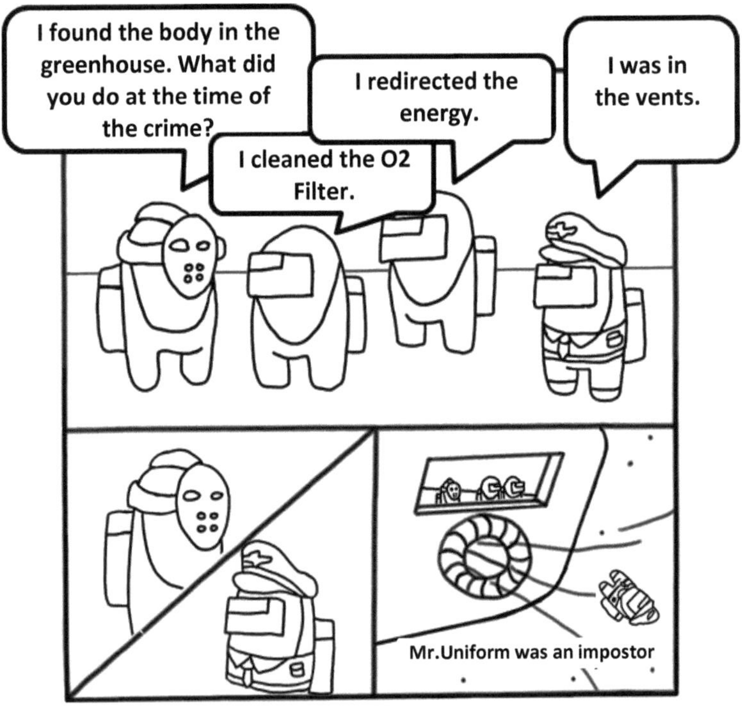

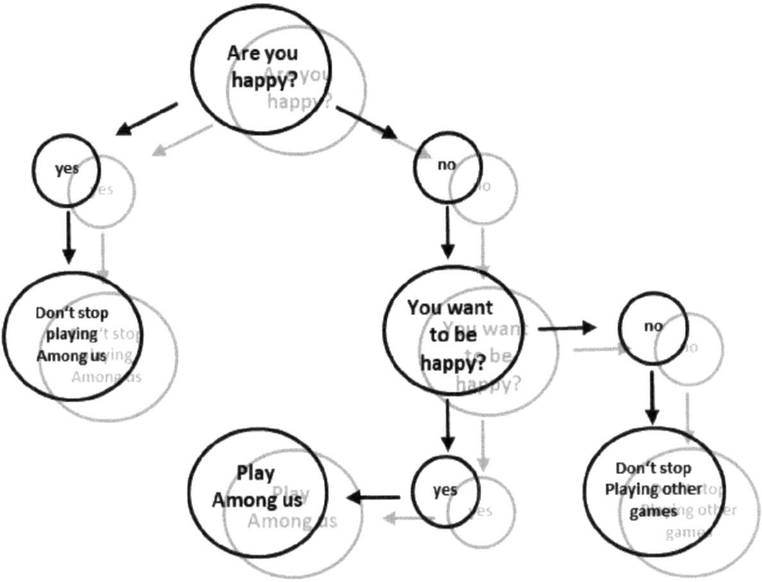

Two Among Us players chat during the session. One of them asks: "Do you know today's date?"

Replies the other:

"Look in the newspaper." Then the first one answers:

"That doesn't help, it's yesterday's."

My Wifi-Connection

When I don't need it

When I search for something in google

When I watch Netflix

When I want to play Among us

I just died and the guy I just picked out:

"Welcome to the realm of shadows, stupid!"

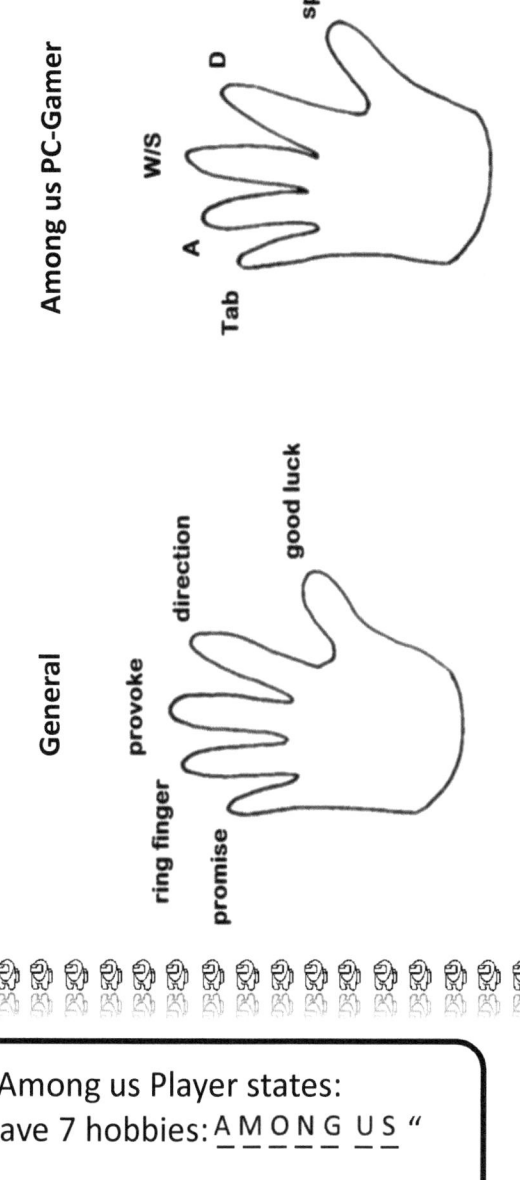

The hand and its meaning

General

- promise
- ring finger
- provoke
- direction
- good luck

Among us PC-Gamer

- Tab
- A
- W/S
- D
- space

An Among us Player states:
„I have 7 hobbies: <u>A</u> <u>M</u> <u>O</u> <u>N</u> <u>G</u> <u>U</u> <u>S</u> "

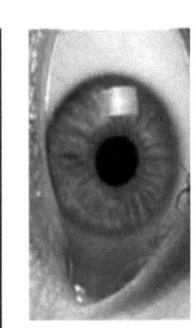

The pupil of the eye can enlarge up to 56% when you see something you love.

The crewmate you voted actually was the impostor and floats around in space after disposal.

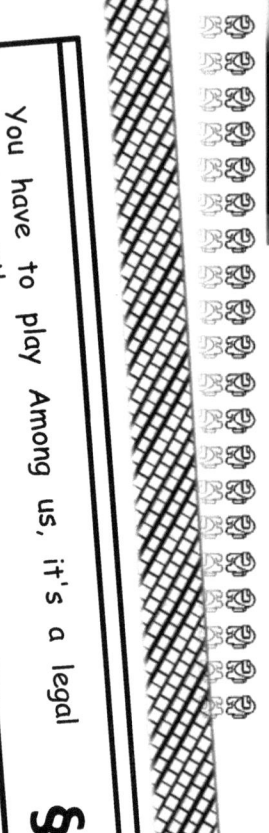

You have to play Among us, it's a legal requirement!

§

Me

„Who is the impostor?"

My Crewmates

Question: What role does Chuck Norris play in Among us?

Answer: He is the fourth impostor.

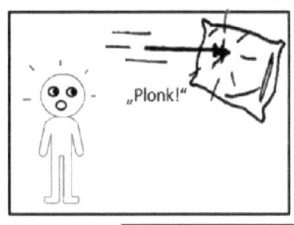

How real Among us fans spend New Year's Eve:

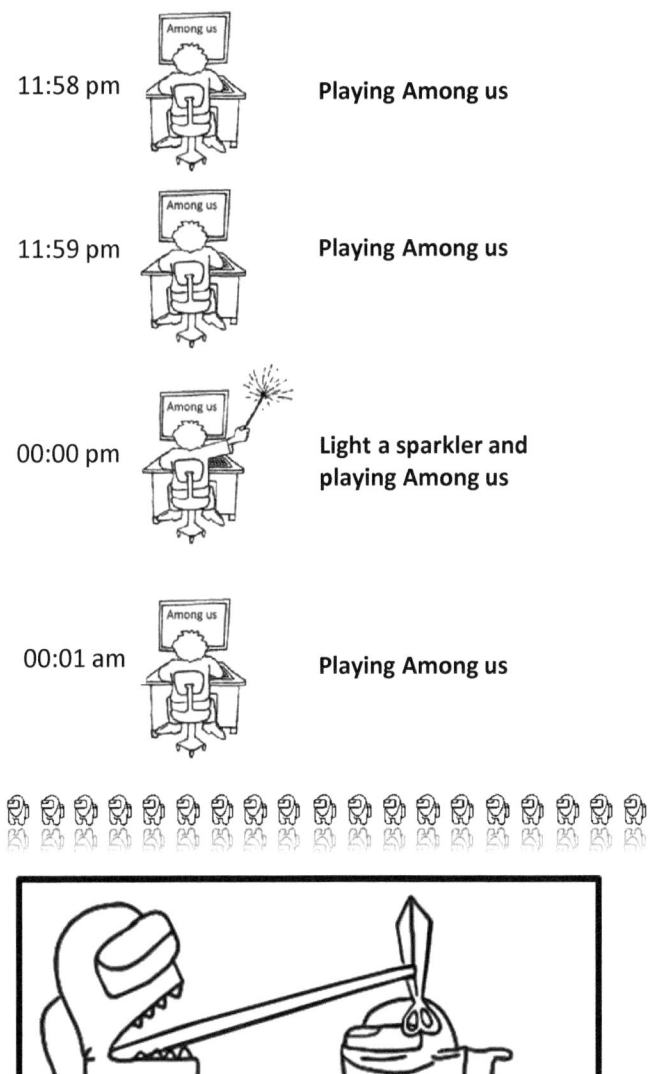

11:58 pm — **Playing Among us**

11:59 pm — **Playing Among us**

00:00 pm — **Light a sparkler and playing Among us**

00:01 am — **Playing Among us**

Typical daily routine of an Among us player:

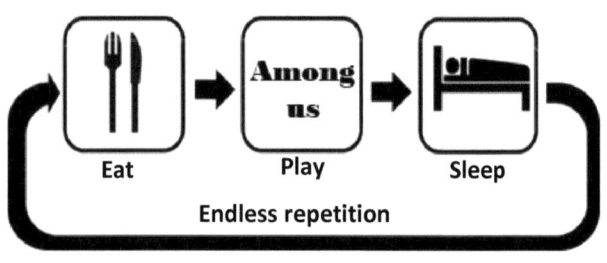

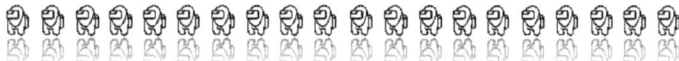

How to upset a Crewmate

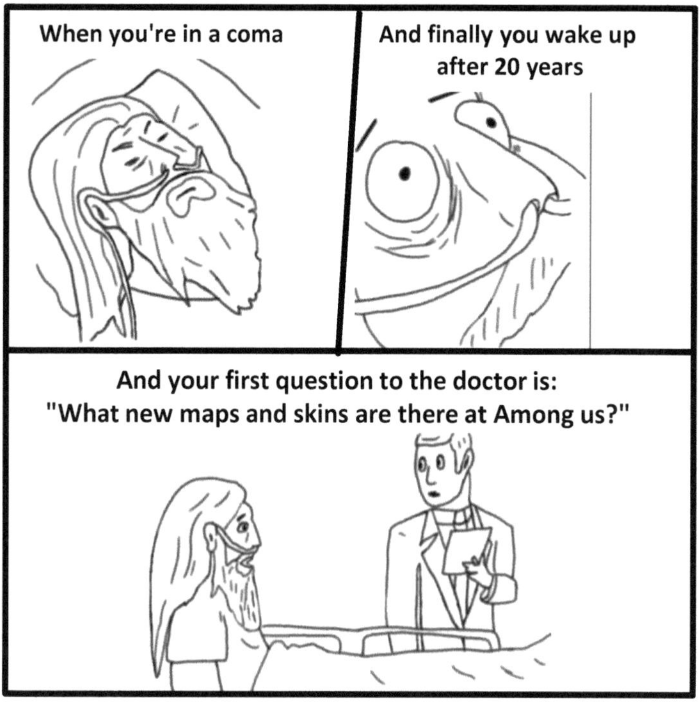

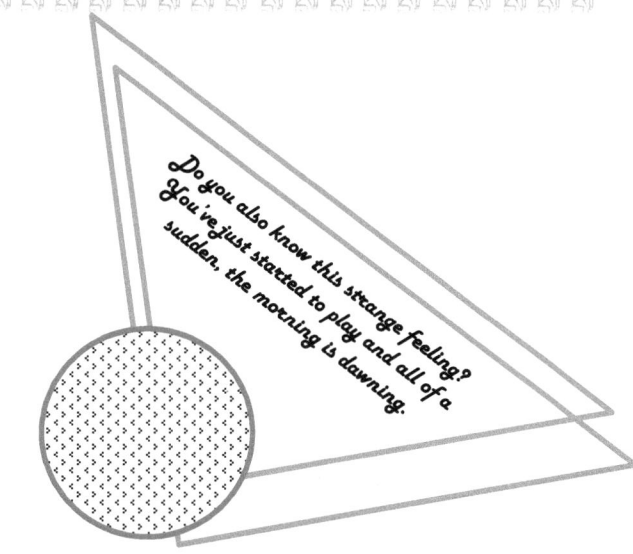

The diffenrent types of headaches

Migraine

High blood pressure

Stress

Doing a task in Electrical

Woman and man lie next to one another in bed.
She thinks: "He's probably thinking of one right now ."

Him dreaming:

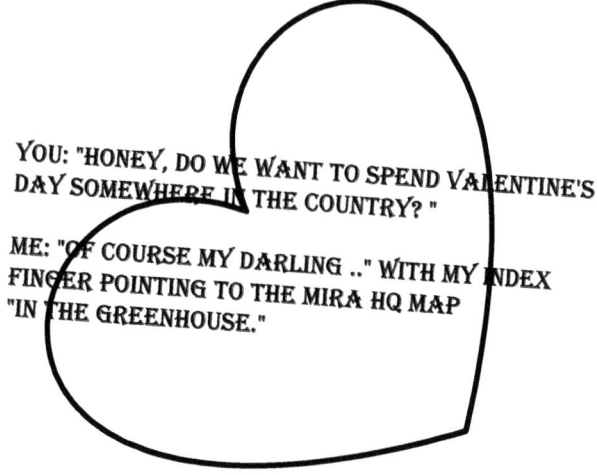

My pulse

In idle state:

When doing sports:

When I am the impostor
in Among us:

Girls

**It's incredible, he didn't cry at
all during this sad movie**

**Maybe he is unable to feel
something?**

Boys

Government statement

"We will halve the homeless by 2026. "

Homeless in 2026:

Recently at the psychologist

Where it hurts the most

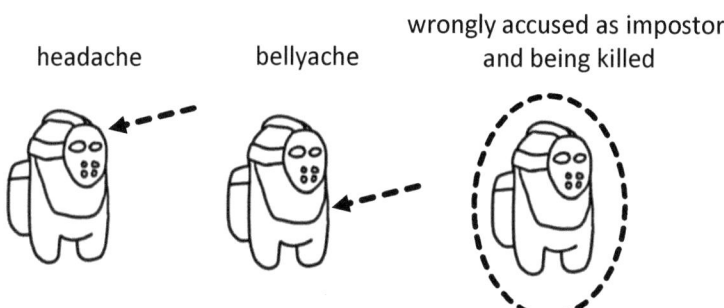

headache

bellyache

wrongly accused as impostor and being killed

When you're the only one on the crew who spends money on a costume.

When you've played Among us about 50 times without being the impostor once.

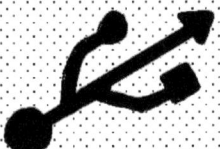

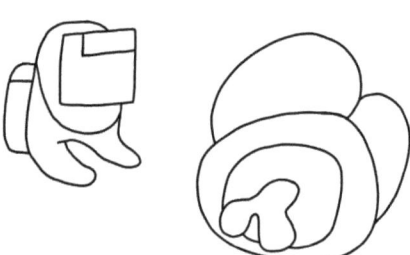

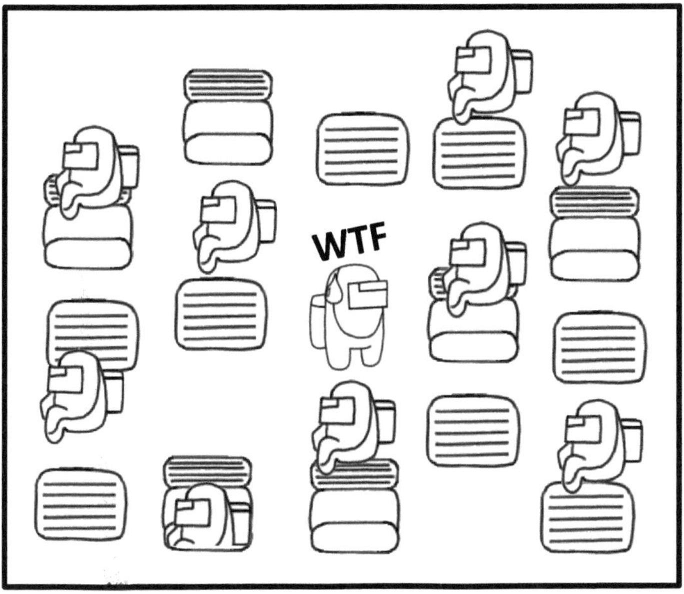

WTF

STAY OUTSIDE!
GAMER AT
★ WORK ★

Killing crew members
Convicting Impostors
Finishing tasks
Doing Votings
Doing fake tasks

PUT FOOD AND DRINK IN FRONT OF THE
DOOR, THEN LEAVE.

ENTRY AT YOUR OWN RISK

Survey among young people between 10 and 35 years of age	
What is more important to you	
To be president	24% (96.015 Votes)
Winning in Among us	76% (303.985 Votes)

If you are one of the last three players
And you were voted as an impostor.

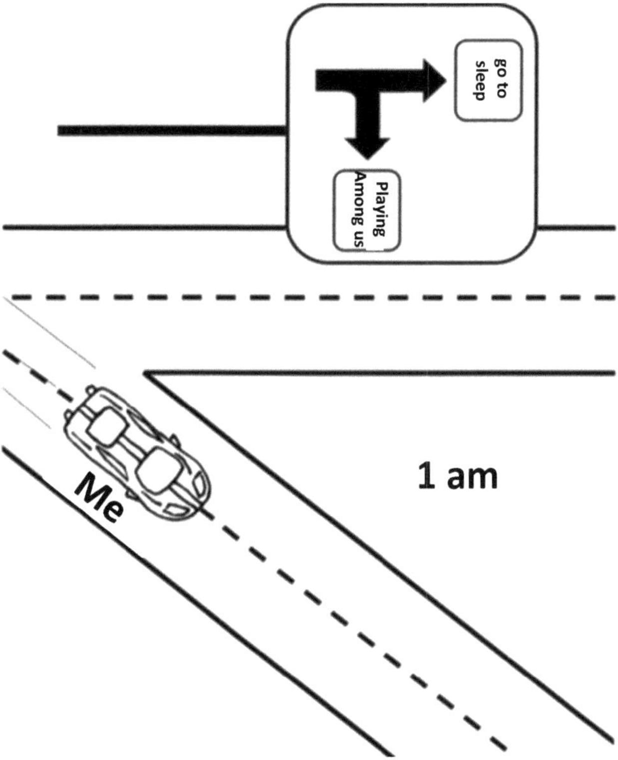

go to
sleep

Playing
Among us

Me

1 am

If your buddy wins the game ...

and he killed you as an impostor ...

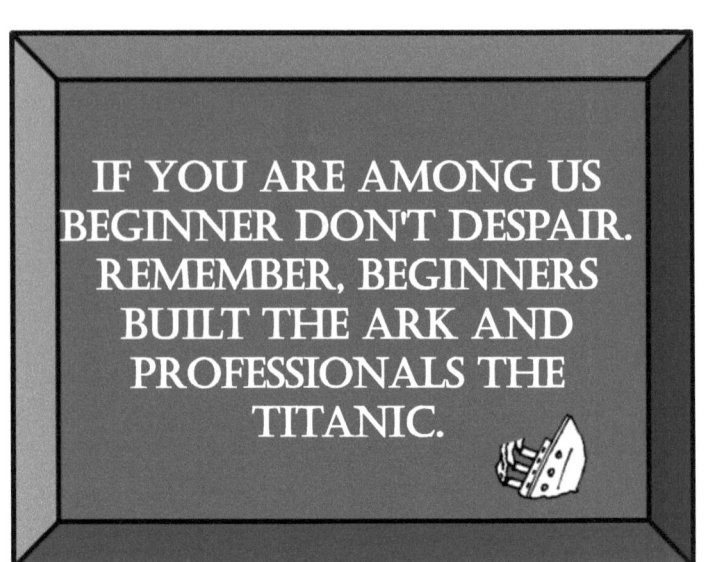

My list of Among us games I won:

Two newbies speak in Among us. One looks around and asks:

"Do you know the way to MedBay?" Replies the other:

"No idea, I'm not from here either."

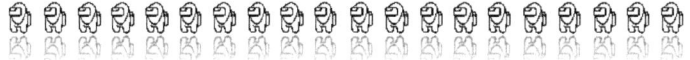

Something that should exist

Your degree

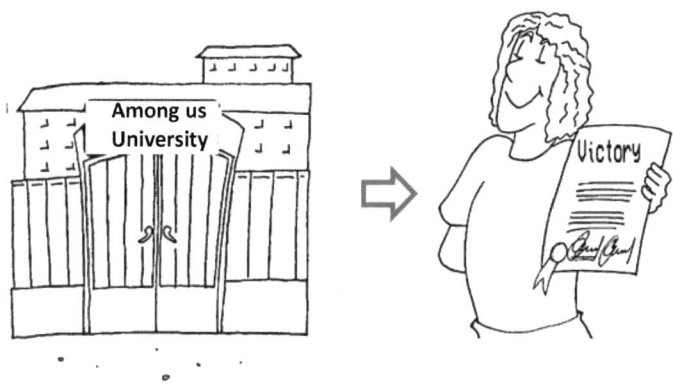

X-ray of a crewmate:

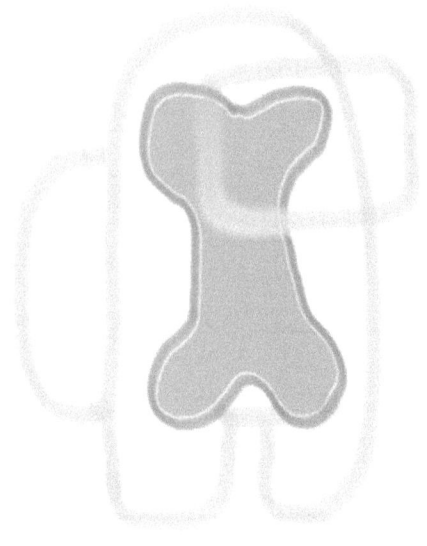

My perfect Christmas

Do you know this feeling?
The time spent without playing Among us?

And you can't figure out
what to do?

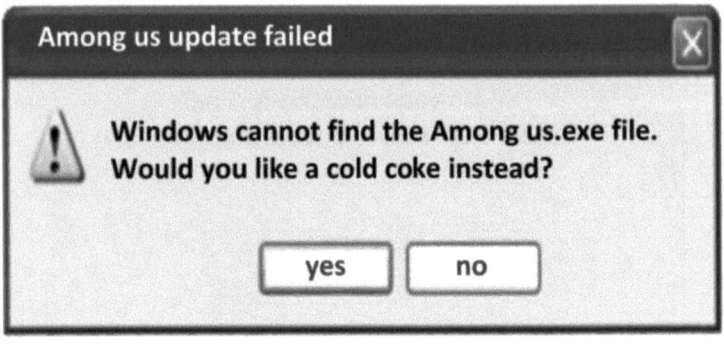

Among us update failed

Windows cannot find the Among us.exe file.
Would you like a cold coke instead?

yes | no

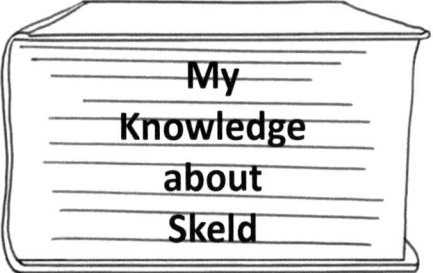

My
Knowledge
about
Skeld

My
School knowledge

New password

> Green disappeared into the ventilation
> Shaft and everyone saw it

Weak

New password

> Don't know, think blue is somehow
> suspicious

Strong

Asscake

Jesus has to die for our sins

Jesus

What, me?

 Ivan has voted. 6 remaining

 Farthaed has voted. 5 remaining

 Bitch has voted. 4 remaining

 Pizza King has voted. 3 remaining

 SchoolLOL has voted. 2 remaining

• • •

Peter to his father before Leaving for his friend's Among us LAN party:

"And dad, what time shall I come home?"

"Ten."

"Ok, shall I bring the newspaper?"

The Impostor has killed you	panic
You are not playing Among us	calm
You are not Playing Among us	panic

Me

Why do you follow me White?

Mr. White

Together we are a zebra

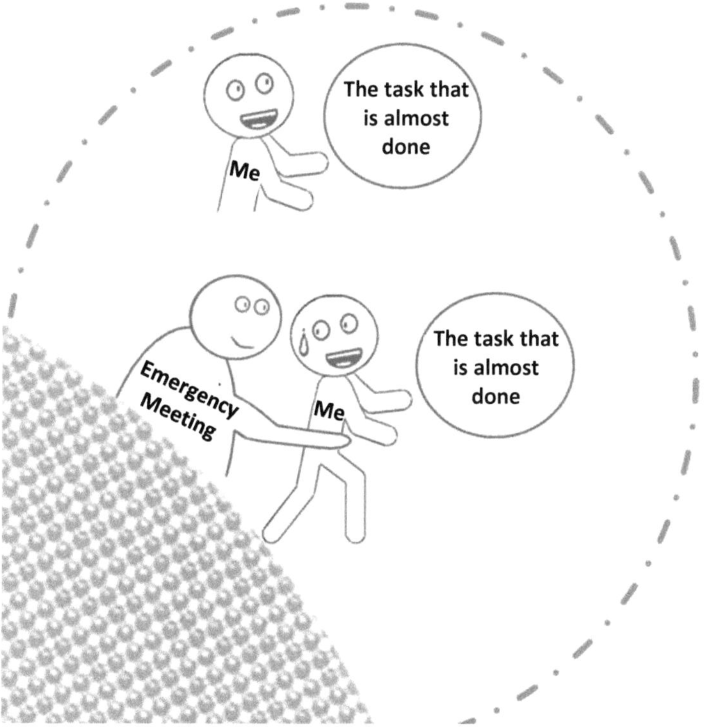

What feature exposes an Among us Gamer?

The red eyes.

If you start the game and you are right away voted as an impostor... but it wasn't you.

When you die	And you want to go to heaven

But God says to you: "First do your tasks!"

How can an Among us Gamer play Among us for 8 days going without sleep?

He sleeps at night.

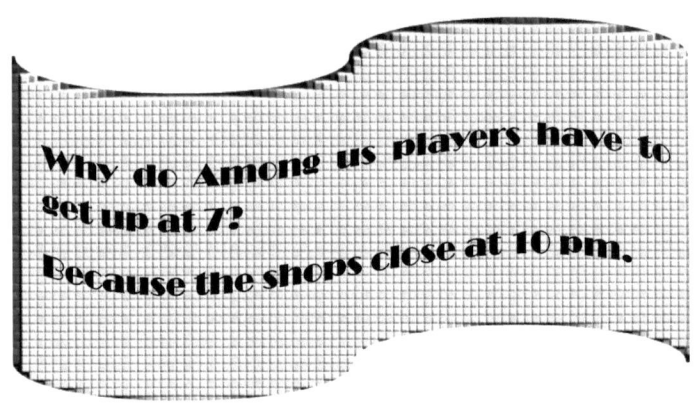

Why do Among us players have to get up at 7?
Because the shops close at 10 pm.

The big AMONGUS

My friends say I'm addicted to Among us. But I always pay attention to a balanced schedule according to importance.

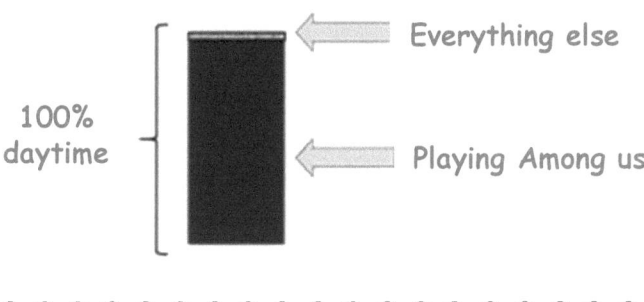

The scariest things in the world

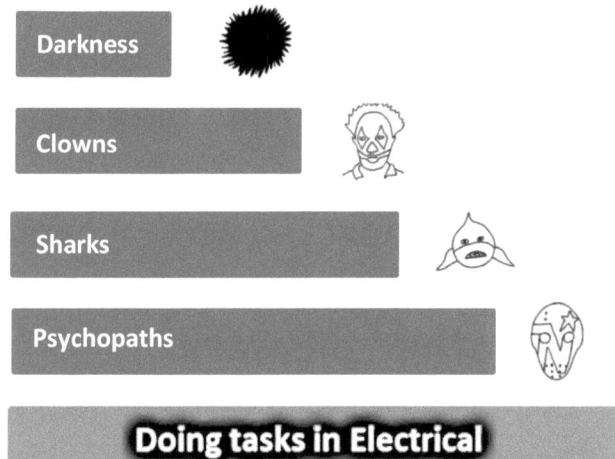

Two Among us Gamers meet after the weekend, one asks:
"And how was your weekend?"
The other answers:
"Light, dark, light, dark, Monday."

A young girl in a depressed mood is standing at the perfume stand of the department store and says to the saleswoman: "Do you have something that smells like Among us?"

When the game starts and you are the impostor

I don't know who or what I am ...

I also don't know where exactly I am ...

But I know one thing for sure, I have to kill!

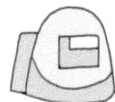

Mr. Mister
We saw you kill Green

Jabber
No, I killed Blue

Me: Putting the clean dishes into the cupboard
My mother: Finding a saucer among the plates

If you liked the book, I would be happy to receive a positive review.